A HISTORICAL ALBUM OF

NEW YORK

A HISTORICAL ALBUM OF
NEW YORK

Monique Avakian   Carter Smith

THE MILLBROOK PRESS, Brookfield, Connecticut

Front and back cover: "The City of New York," lithograph by Charles Parsons, published by Currier & Ives, 1856. Library of Congress.

Title page: Watkins Glen, Seneca Lake. Courtesy of New York State Department of Economic Development.

Library of Congress Cataloging-in-Publication Data

Avakian, Monique
    A historical album of New York / Monique Avakian & Carter Smith III.
      p. cm. — (Historical albums)
    Includes bibliographical references and index.
    Summary: Surveys the history of New York State, from pre-colonial times through its industrial, political, and social development to current economic and environmental concerns. Gazetteer includes map, statistics, and other facts.
    ISBN 1-56294-005-8 (lib. bdg.)
    1. New York (State)—History—Juvenile literature. [1. New York (State)—History.] I. Smith, Carter, 1962– . II. Title.
III. Series.
F119.3.A93 1993
974.7—dc20
                                         92-41135
                                           CIP
                                           AC

Created in association with Media Projects Incorporated

    C. Carter Smith, *Executive Editor*
    Lelia Wardwell, *Managing Editor*
    Monique Avakian and Carter Smith III, *Principal Writers*
    Andrea Geller, *Designer*
    Shelley Latham, *Picture Researcher*
    Carl Jablonski, *Cartographer*

    Consultant: Lester John Szabo, Teacher Education Associate, Buffalo Research Institute on Education for Teaching, State University of New York at Buffalo.

10 9 8 7 6 5 4 3 2 1

CONTENTS

Introduction

Both New York's land and its people are among the most diverse in the nation. A visitor to the state can see both human-made wonders, such as the skyscrapers of New York City, and scenes of great natural beauty, including the Hudson River Highlands and Niagara Falls. New York is second only to California in population, but a big part of the state—the Adirondack State Park—contains vast stretches of near-wilderness. A gateway for immigrants since the 17th century, New York City remains a community where you can hear almost any language in the world being spoken.

New York's geography has shaped its history. Located in the middle of North America's Atlantic Coast, the region was a crossroads for many Native American groups in the centuries before European explorers reached its shores. In the early 1600s, the Dutch arrived in the area, starting colonies at Fort Orange (later Albany) and New Amsterdam (now New York City). After control of the region passed to Britain, New York City, with its magnificent harbor, became one of North America's leading ports.

New York's power and influence continued to grow in the 19th century. The Erie Canal, opened in 1825, linked the Great Lakes to New York Harbor. The canal helped spur the development not only of New York, but the entire country.

New York is nicknamed "the Empire State" because it has been a leader in many fields. Despite the challenges of recent decades—inner city poverty, economic slumps, and pollution, to name just a few—the state still plays a leading role in the life of the nation, and the world.

PART ONE

LEADING A NEW NATION

New York City was the nation's first capital, and Federal Hall was its statehouse. As the largest and most promising city in America, New York stood as a hopeful symbol for the new nation.

New York played an important role in early American history. Long before there was a United States, the region was home to the Iroquois League, one of the most powerful Native American groups in North America. In colonial times, its waterways—especially the Hudson River and the great harbor at its mouth—made it a flourishing center for trade. After the American Revolution, New York State and New York City grew by leaps and bounds. And with the opening of the Erie Canal in 1825, the state gained new importance as a gateway between the Atlantic Coast and the Western states and territories.

New York Before the Europeans

People first came to New York more than 10,000 years ago. The first Americans traveled into North America from Asia, by way of a land bridge that once connected the two continents. We know these groups as Native Americans, or Indians. The Native American tribes in the New York area fell into two groups: the Algonquians and the Iroquois.

The Algonquians arrived first. They lived and hunted throughout most of the area. When the Iroquois moved in from the north in about A.D.1300, they pushed the Algonquians into southeastern New York.

Until 1570, the Iroquois tribes fought among themselves. They argued over boundaries and over hunting and fishing rights. Under the leadership of Hiawatha, however, the five tribes (named the Senecas, Cayugas, Onondagas, Oneidas, and Mohawks) put aside their differences and joined together.

This group became the League of Five Nations. It was the first democracy created in North America. Although each of the five tribes went on governing itself, the League created a council of about fifty chiefs. Each member of the council was called a sachem. They met each year to settle disputes both among the tribes and with outside enemies.

Benjamin Franklin, one of America's founding fathers, had great respect for the League of Five Nations. He encouraged America's leaders to study the group closely. The government of the United States today has much in common with the way the Iroquois League was organized. For example, although under a federal government, each state keeps its own local government.

Iroquois women were highly respected and had great power within the tribe. They owned property, settled family problems, chose tribal chiefs, and directed political meetings. When a couple married, they went to live with the woman's family, and the children were given her clan name.

Corn was an essential food for most Indian groups in the East. Iroquois women were in charge of farming as well as gathering wild nuts and berries. Iroquois women worked the soil with hoes made of wood and antlers. They planted five or six seeds of corn in mounds of dirt set about two feet apart. When the corn came up, bean and squash seeds were put in right next to them. After about ten years of this kind of farming, the soil would become infertile. The tribe would then move to another spot of land, leaving their homes behind.

As in most societies, women were

This painting shows Atoharo, chief of the Onondaga nation, with snakes encircling his body. When Hiawatha convinced the warlike Onondaga chief to make peace, the League of Five Nations was born.

The totem of the Iroquois League (left) shows a strong central circle in the middle with four stags facing outward. The League of Five Nations was the first democratic government in North America.

also responsible for raising the children. Babies were wrapped in moss diapers and carried on their mothers' backs in cradle boards.

Iroquois boys of six or seven were taught how to use a small bow and arrow, and at nine or ten were shown how to hunt small game, such as rabbits and chipmunks. Iroquois girls learned to grind corn, keep house, cook, sew, and look after the babies.

All children attended ceremonies and festivals. Six times each year the Iroquois put together festivals to make sure that the seasons would be good to them. At gatherings such as the Maple Festival and Corn Planting Festival, men and women would chant, dance, and offer sacrifices to the Great Spirit.

In warm weather, men usually wore just moccasins, leggings, and breech cloths (leather wrappings that came to the knees). Women wore moccasins, leggings, and deerskin skirts that fell below the knees. In cold weather men added a tunic-like shirt with fringed edges, and women added a fringed cape-like blouse.

Iroquois men hunted with stone clubs, blow guns, and bows and arrows for deer, bear, moose, beaver, wild turkey, and other game. Bone hooks, traps, and nets were used for fishing. The men also cleared the land and made tools, weapons, and elm-bark canoes. The heavy Iroquois canoes, however, were not nearly as speedy as the well-made Algonquian birchbark canoes. In fact, the Iroquois stole Algonquian canoes whenever possible.

Iroquois men showed great skill as warriors, too. They were regarded as the fiercest Native American warriors north of Mexico. In 1634, William Wood, a Plymouth settler, described a group of attacking Mohawks as screaming: "Hadree Hadree succomee succomee, we come we come to sucke your blood . . . "

Unlike the Algonquians, who lived in dome-shaped houses called "wigwams," the Iroquois lived in barn-shaped homes called "longhouses." The longhouse could be anywhere from 50 to 150 feet long and 18 to 25 feet wide. Each longhouse sheltered as many as twenty families.

Each family had its own section about as big as a large bunk bed. Beds were made of strips of bark. Pillows, blankets, mattresses, and curtains were fashioned out of animal skins. Possessions were stored under the beds and on shelves up above.

Fires for cooking and heating were made in the middle aisle that ran the length of the house. There were no windows in the longhouse. Smoke escaped through holes in the roof made of elm bark. During the winter, moss was stuffed into the cracks of the bark walls to keep out the cold.

Iroquois villages were well defended. Unlike the Algonquians, the Iroquois usually built their homes on hilltops so they could see enemy movements. Each village was surrounded with a tall fence made of logs with sharpened points. Warriors would stand on a platform behind the wall near the top and shoot arrows down at invaders. A big ditch was dug around the stockade so that it would be even more difficult for their enemies to reach them. The forts European settlers built copied many of these features.

Like other Native Americans, the Iroquois believed that the surprise attack was the best way to fight. The night before a raid, the war chief would summon the village warriors to a ceremony where they danced and prayed to prepare for battle.

In the early 1600s, the Iroquois ruled the land from present-day Montreal, Canada, through New York and into Pennsylvania. All this would change over the next 200 years, as the European colonists arrived and moved into the territory.

Women played an important role in Iroquois society. As leaders of the clans, they had the right to choose which men would attend meetings of the League (above, right).

Iroquois men were known to be fierce and able warriors. This one (right) holds a tomahawk in his right hand and carries an ax in his belt.

Sauvage Iroquois

Exploration and Settlement

The excellent bay and harbor at the mouth of the Hudson River, as well as the promising fur trade, lured European explorers and settlers to the area. The first explorer to visit the New York region was probably Giovanni da Verrazano. He sailed his ship into New York Bay in 1524.

In 1609, Samuel de Champlain, who worked for France, came south from Canada. The lake that now borders New York, Vermont, and Canada was discovered and named Lake Champlain during this trip.

In September 1609, Henry Hudson sailed into New York Bay. He traveled up a broad river that would soon bear his name, north to the site of Albany. He then claimed the surrounding land for Holland.

Although some Native Americans were unfriendly to the newcomers, others were interested in trading furs for cloth, tools, and weapons. Many of the explorers who came to North America were also involved in the fur trade. They built trading posts where they did business with trappers and Indians. As more people came to the New World, they built settlements around these trading posts.

The Dutch West India Company, formed in 1621, took advantage of the fur trade. This company played a big part in the founding of the Dutch

The game of bowling was one of the many traditions Americans inherited from the Dutch. Others include the painting of Easter eggs and the hanging of stockings at Christmas.

colony along the Hudson River, named New Netherland. In 1624 the company invited about thirty families from Holland to settle in the area. Some went north and founded Fort Orange (now Albany). The following year, colonists built a town on Manhattan Island and named it New Amsterdam (now New York City).

The colony's governor, Peter Minuit, arrived in May 1626. Minuit bought the island of Manhattan from a tribe of Canarsee Indians. He presented a trunkful of trinkets, beads, cloth, and knives worth approximately $24 (according to legend).

The Dutch set up a patroon (landowner) system in the colony in 1629. Landowners encouraged families to live on their property and raise crops and animals. The farmers would pay the landowner with a portion of their earnings.

The colonists of New Amsterdam were at first mainly fur traders, farmers, and soldiers. As the colony grew into a permanent settlement, merchants, teachers, lawyers, and various craftsmen began moving in.

Tensions between the Indians and the European settlers increased as the colonists took over more and more of the land where the Indians had been living for centuries. A new governor, William Kieft, made matters worse.

He decided to tax the Indians. In revenge, the Indians attacked the settlers. During the next two years, colonists moved into the fort at New Amsterdam for safety. After losing

hundreds of people in battle, the Algonquians agreed to a peace treaty, ending Kieft's Indian war in 1645.

Peter Stuyvesant was sent to the colony in 1647. He was called "Peg Leg Pete" or "Old Silver Leg" behind his back because of his wooden leg.

Stuyvesant ruled the people harshly. When the colonists threatened to complain he replied, "If anyone during my administration shall appeal, I will make him a foot shorter and send the pieces to Holland and let him appeal in that way!"

Stuyvesant did bring law and order to the colony, however, and made peace with the Algonquians. He was the last Dutch governor. In 1664, an English army came to New Netherland to take over the colony.

The fur trade played a major role in the growth of New Netherland. This meeting (above) between white trappers and Native Americans shows how cooperation between the two groups was necessary for success of the fur trade.

This row of tall, narrow houses (opposite page), typical for the Dutch, was built in Fort Orange (now Albany). Although the French were active in New York's fur trade, the Dutch were the first to build permanent settlements there.

Under British Rule

Although the English colonists had once gotten along with the Dutch, the two groups gradually came to oppose each other. King Charles II of England took action in May 1664, when he sent a fleet to seize New Netherland.

Stuyvesant asked for help, but the Dutch West India Company refused to send more money and soldiers. The company did not consider New Netherland an important colony. So when the British warships came into New York Harbor, Stuyvesant had no choice but to surrender.

The English renamed the territory New York after the king's brother James, the Duke of York. New York lay between the English holdings in Virginia and Massachusetts. Now England controlled the whole area. By the early 1700s, the entire east coast (except for Florida) was under England's rule.

In the late 1680s, England was in a period of turmoil. King James II was removed from the throne in 1688. The colonies joined the rebellion by rejecting the governor of New England, Sir Edmund Andros. Jacob Leisler led a rebel army and threw out Francis Nicholson, the English governor of New York. Leisler named himself governor of the colony in 1689.

Leisler made sure the people were taxed fairly. Under his rule, more citizens could vote and hold public posts.

Officials in England did not approve of Leisler's actions. King William III sent Henry Sloughter to take Leisler's place. Leisler refused to surrender and was arrested for treason (going against the state). On May 16, 1691, Leisler and his son-in-law were sentenced to death by hanging.

There were others in New York who continued to challenge authority. One man, John Peter Zenger, expressed his views through the press instead of force. In 1733, Zenger started a newspaper called the New York *Weekly Journal*. He wanted to rival William Bradford's New York *Gazette*. Zenger felt that the *Gazette* printed views that supported only those of New York's wealthy merchants and Governor William Cosby.

Zenger's *Journal* made fun of New York officials by showing them as lost animals in phony ads. The sheriff, for example, was pictured as "a monkey of the larger sort, about four feet high." The paper was popular among working class New Yorkers.

Governor Cosby burned copies of the paper in public and had Zenger thrown in jail for treason. While Zenger was in jail, his wife continued the paper. They discussed matters

"I would [rather] have been carried to my grave," said Peter Stuyvesant upon surrendering New York to the British in 1664. This engraving shows the Dutch governor angrily agreeing to give over the colony.

through a hole in the prison door.

The Zenger trial of 1735 was an important victory for freedom of the press. The odds of winning were against Zenger, mainly because Judge James De Lancey was a good friend of Governor Cosby's. When Zenger's lawyers complained, the governor took away their licenses to practice law. Then Zenger's friends managed to hire the famous lawyer Andrew Hamilton to represent him. Zenger was found not guilty.

New Yorkers were also involved in conflicts beyond their colony and they supported Britain in its struggle with France for control of North America. Britain and France, and their Indian allies, fought in a series of wars during the late 17th and 18th centuries. The conflicts are known as the French and Indian Wars. New York was a key territory throughout the struggle.

After England won control of southern New York, the French, who held territory in Canada, wanted the northern part. In 1731, they built a fort at Crown Point on Lake Champlain. Crown Point, as well as French-controlled Fort Niagara and Fort Ticonderoga, became significant battlefields in New York.

By 1754, hopes for a British victory seemed dim. The French were winning most of the battles. Also, Britain's main Indian allies, the Iroquois, were thinking about ending the partnership. That year, an emergency meeting was called at Albany. Representatives from Massachusetts, Rhode Island, Connecticut, New York, New Hampshire, Pennsylvania, Maryland,

and the Iroquois League attended this meeting, now known as the Albany Congress. Benjamin Franklin urged the colonies to join together for their protection. A New Yorker named Sir William Johnson managed to convince the Iroquois to stay with the British. In the summer of 1759, Britain captured the key forts at Niagara, Ticonderoga, and Crown Point. With the help of its Iroquois allies, Britain was able to triumph over France.

The Peace of Paris, signed in 1763, ended the struggle for control of North America. Britain was victorious. France lost almost all of its possessions on the continent.

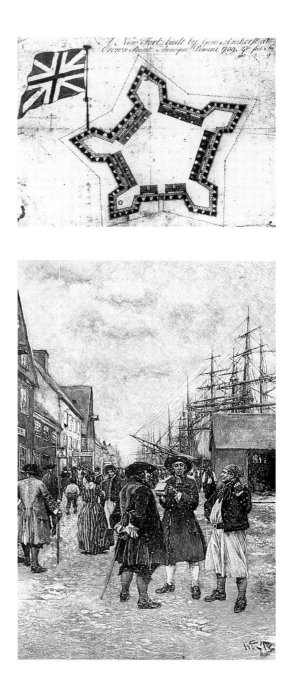

Fort Johnson (opposite page) was an important trading center and meeting place for whites and Indians.

The French built this fort (above, right) on Lake Champlain in 1731. The layout was star-shaped so that the defenders could fire at approaching troops from many different angles. The British succeeded in capturing the fort, named Crown Point, in 1759.

The British ruled the colonies with strict laws and heavy taxes. Some colonists, like the merchants meeting on the New York City waterfront in this illustration (right), turned to piracy and smuggling in order to import goods more cheaply.

New York and the Revolution

The American colonists fought the major battles of the Revolutionary War from 1775 to 1781 in the hope of gaining their independence from Britain. New Yorkers played a very important role in the conflict.

New York City was a center of revolutionary activity before the war started. In the 1760s and 1770s, the colonists formed local groups, called the Sons of Liberty, to protest the new taxes Britain was imposing. The Stamp Act of 1765 caused the greatest anger because it taxed all printed matter, such as newspapers and legal documents. The Stamp Act Congress met in New York City in 1765. After the members decided to refuse to buy all British goods, Parliament finally canceled the act. Protests continued when the Townshend Acts were passed in 1767.

When the war began, not all New Yorkers supported the Patriots. Some were neutral, hoping that the conflict would end quickly. Others, known as Loyalists, or Tories, sided with Brittain. Of the thirteen colonies, New York had the most Loyalists.

During the Revolutionary War, nearly 45,000 New Yorkers took up arms. One third of the war's battles were fought in New York. At the start of the war, the Patriots captured the two forts on Lake Champlain, Crown

Although the fire of September 20, 1776, was probably accidental, it could have been a last-ditch effort to force the British to give up control of New York City. Throughout the Revolutionary War, New York remained a Loyalist stronghold.

Point and Fort Ticonderoga from the British.

Britain's main strategy was to split New England from the southern colonies. New York's location was important in this plan. New York's harbor was also an ideal landing base for British troops. In April 1776, General George Washington arrived with Patriot troops.

But Washington failed to hold onto New York City. In a series of battles between August and November 1776, the British succeeded in seizing the city and the entire island of Manhat-tan from the Patriots. New York City remained under Redcoat control for the rest of the war. Thousands of Tory colonists moved there.

The Patriots still held upstate New York—for the time being. In 1776, British general John Burgoyne was ordered to sweep down through the Hudson River Valley from Canada to invade the colonies.

Burgoyne recaptured Fort Ticon-deroga on July 6, 1777. But he was defeated at Bennington, Vermont, on August 16. By September, Burgoyne's dwindling forces were stranded near

Saratoga. They encountered the Patriots in a series of battles at Freeman's Farm. Outnumbered three to one, Burgoyne surrendered to American general Horatio Gates at Saratoga on October 17.

The rest of the war took place in the South, but the years 1778–81 were marked by great violence in the North. Loyalists and Iroquois brutally attacked settlers in New York and Pennsylvania in 1778. Washington sent forces to take revenge the following year. They destroyed Iroquois crops and villages so completely that the Iroquois never regained their powerful position in the area.

French and American forces defeated the British at Yorktown, Virginia, on October 19, 1781. A peace treaty was signed two years later, recognizing the independence of the states from England. The last British soldiers left New York City on November 25, 1783.

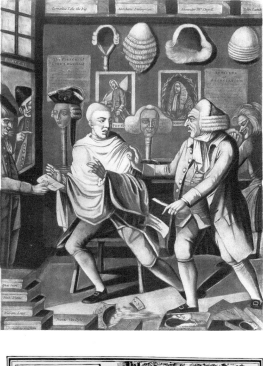

This engraving (opposite page) shows General John Burgoyne's army, low on supplies and stranded at Saratoga, New York, in 1777.

This cartoon (above, right), published in New York in 1774, shows a patriotic barber chasing a British soldier out of his shop. Anti-British feeling spread throughout the colonies as more citizens called for independence.

West Point (right) was a key post in the American defense of the Hudson River during the Revolutionary War. Traitor Benedict Arnold planned to sell plans of the fort to the British in 1780.

Constitution and Statehood

New York adopted its first constitution in 1777. But the new nation was in danger of splitting apart, with no president, no courts, and no way to tax the people. A Constitutional Convention was held in Philadelphia in 1787 in order to create a stronger central government.

Many New Yorkers did not want the federal government to have more power. But a group called the Federalists (because they wanted a strong federal government) helped convince many New Yorkers to support the new Constitution. In a close vote, New York accepted the document on July 26, 1788, and became the nation's eleventh state. New York City was the nation's capital from 1785 to 1790. On April 30, 1789, in New York, George Washington was sworn in as America's first president.

For Indians in New York, the end of the Revolution and the beginning of statehood brought great changes. The once-powerful Iroquois never fully recovered from the damage they suffered in the war. A series of treaties made between 1784 and 1822 with the new American government sealed the final defeat for this tribe.

New York enjoyed a period of peace and prosperity until 1812, when war against Britain erupted again. The War of 1812 was fought

Federalists such as Alexander Hamilton (above) convinced many New Yorkers that the new nation needed a strong central government to survive.

This is an early draft of the Bill of Rights: The twelve amendments shown here (left) became ten in the final version. New Yorkers fought especially hard to have these amendments added to the Constitution. They protect the freedom of the press, speech, and religion, among other rights.

mainly because of British shipping laws that many Americans felt harmed their foreign trade. Much of the fighting occurred in the frontier regions near the New York-Canadian border. America's only two significant naval victories took place near New York: one by Oliver Hazard Perry on Lake Erie, September 10, 1813; and one by Thomas MacDonough on Lake Champlain, September 11, 1814. At the war's end in 1814, neither side had made major gains, but both sides claimed victory.

The war resulted in another crushing defeat for the Indians. Tecumseh, chief of the Shawnee tribe, had brought together thirty-two tribes. They joined with the British and fought against American settlers who were moving into the western frontier. When Tecumseh was killed by American forces in 1813, the alliance between the Indians and the British was destroyed. As a result, the northern and western frontiers in New York State were opened for settlers.

Many people came to New York because the farmland was better, and taxes were not as high. But traveling about this large area was difficult. There were very few roads on the

frontier, just cleared trails. Rivers were the only way to travel long distances. To help people settle the land, New York needed new roads. In 1797, New York's first hard-surfaced road was built. It ran fifteen miles from Albany to Schenectady, and cost $10,000 per mile. Travelers on this road, which was called a turnpike, were required to pay a toll. Over the next several decades many more of these turnpikes were built. By 1821 there were about 4,000 miles of road throughout the state.

Probably the most important invention of the early 19th century was the steam-powered engine. In 1807, a steamboat built by Robert Fulton traveled the 150-mile route along the Hudson River from New York City to Albany in thirty-two hours.

Steam power changed New York forever. It allowed factories to be built, which could produce more goods than ever before. These factories needed to be near good transportation routes in order to grow and prosper. Steam-powered factories had to be close to waterways. And as they grew, they needed larger amounts of fuel, generally coal. Also, because they were making so many more goods than before, businesses had to find more places to sell their products. In 1825, a major transportation project, the Erie Canal, was completed. It brought tremendous success to many businesses in New York State.

In this 19th-century engraving, Robert Fulton's ship, the *Clermont*, steams past the towering cliffs known as the Palisades, just north of New York City on the Hudson River. Within a decade, steamboats would be a common sight on New York's waterways.

In a fierce three-hour battle on September 10, 1813, an American fleet commanded by Captain Oliver Hazard Perry drove British warships from Lake Erie (opposite page). Control of Lake Erie, a gateway to New York, was an important goal of both sides during the War of 1812.

The Erie Canal

The Erie Canal was started in Rome, New York, on July 4th, 1817, and took eight years to build. When finished, it connected the Hudson River to Lake Erie in a single waterway.

De Witt Clinton, governor of New York, was the one who made the canal happen. He was New York's most powerful politician. The nephew of George Clinton, the state's first governor, he had also been mayor of New York City for many years.

Clinton believed that a waterway across the entire state would lower the cost of bringing goods from one part of the state to another. Since building the canal was expected to be very expensive, however, most New Yorkers were against the idea. Some opponents of the canal even named it "Clinton's Ditch." Even so, Clinton still managed to get the state government to approve the project.

On October 26, 1825, the canal opened. A fleet of twenty-six boats set out from Buffalo with Clinton in the lead boat, the *Seneca Chief.* One of the other boats was called *Noah's Ark.* It carried animals, birds, and several fish. Cannons placed along the canal were fired to announce the canal's opening. Crowds cheered the boats at every stop. On November 4, Clinton poured a keg of water from Lake Erie into New York Harbor to celebrate the opening of the waterway.

The canal was a great success. The

cost of shipping a ton of freight from Buffalo to New York City fell from $100 to $6. This was a boon to New York farmers. It was cheaper, for example, to bring wheat from New York to Savannah, Georgia, by water than it was to bring Georgia-grown wheat by land into Savannah.

The new canal also helped settlers move from the eastern part of the state to the west. Many new towns and cities sprouted up along the canal's route through central and western New York. After 1825, many more canals were built, making transportation even easier.

The Erie Canal also made it easier to sell goods overseas. By 1831, half of all the goods coming into the country from overseas passed through New York. Almost one third of all goods leaving the United States to be sold in other countries also passed through the state. Business boomed in the canal towns of Utica, Syracuse, Rochester, and Buffalo.

The skeptics who had grumbled about "Clinton's Ditch" now sang the canal's praises. Within a few years, tolls on the boats that traveled the canal more than paid back the cost of its construction. As one writer said, "They [Clinton and the canal builders] have built the longest canal in the world in the least time, with the least experience, for the least money, and for the greatest public benefit."

Towns along the Erie Canal marked its opening with parades and celebrations. This print (above) shows a float built by firemen of the "Clinton Fire Company" taking part in one such parade. The print also shows a boat passing through one of the waterway's many locks.

This illustration (opposite) shows boats carrying people and cargo on the Erie Canal shortly after it was opened in 1825. The new canal, which made transportation faster and cheaper, helped New York to grow into the country's richest state.

PART TWO

INDUSTRY AND GROWTH

When the Brooklyn Bridge—the largest suspension bridge in the world—was opened in 1883, New Yorkers celebrated with a fireworks display.

Since the opening of the Erie Canal, New York has been through many changes, moving from farming to factories and then to computers and communications. Through it all, New York City has always been the country's financial center. Many people who have come to America from around the world have arrived in New York. In the 1840s, Germans and Irish came, followed later by Italians and Eastern Europeans. More recently people from the Caribbean, Asia, and other parts of the world have come to New York. Today's New York faces many problems, including a changing economy, poverty, pollution, and racial tension. As the state moves toward the 21st century, its citizens will again be called upon for new answers.

From Farms to Factories

By the start of the 19th century, New York was well on its way toward becoming the financial center of the America. In fact, New York City would soon pass both Boston and Philadelphia as the nation's largest port. Even during colonial times, the city was a major trade center for foreign ports. Banking became very important. In 1792, one of the most important business meetings ever took place. Twenty-four New Yorkers met on Wall Street in downtown Manhattan and set rules for buying and selling stocks and bonds. The New York Stock Exchange was born.

It allowed people to invest their money by buying and selling "shares" in companies.

In the new century, several other developments helped New York grow. The state's first railroad, the Mohawk and Hudson line, began running on August 9, 1831. A locomotive made its first trip from Albany to Schenectady. Soon new train lines were added throughout the state.

The West Point Foundry at Cold Spring (below) was located in the Hudson River Valley. It was one of many new factories that opened in New York State in the first half of the 19th century.

By the early 1850s, the same towns that had grown because of the Erie Canal—Buffalo, Rochester, Syracuse, and Utica—got another big boost. Erastus Corning, a businessman from Albany, formed a big railroad by combining smaller ones. It ran from Buffalo to Albany. Before long, other networks connected Albany to New York City. Together with the canal, the railroad brought in goods from across the country to be shipped overseas.

In addition to banking and shipping, several new trades were thriving in other cities around the state. One was the textile (cloth) trade. Cotton was grown mainly in the South, and sent North to be made into cloth. New York's first cotton mill was built in 1804 in Washington County. Before long, other mills were built in Oneida, Columbia, Dutchess, and Saratoga counties.

Then Elias Howe created the first sewing machine in 1845, and the garment industry was born. With the sewing machine, workers could now make clothes much faster and in much larger quantities than ever before. Many clothing factories sprang up in New York City.

Another popular trade was making metals. Many New Yorkers worked in mines near Lake Champlain and in the state's central region. The iron they found was used for stoves, plows, nails, and other items. The city of Troy became a center for the iron industry when Henry Burden, a Scottish immigrant in Troy, invented a machine that made horseshoes and railroad spikes. Other iron-products companies were located in New York City. In 1854, the first building made with iron girders was built there—a forerunner to the skyscrapers.

Other industries also grew throughout the state. Syracuse was nicknamed "Salt City" because it produced so much salt. Many farmers worked as lumberjacks in the Adirondack, Catskill, and Allegheny mountains during the fall and winter. Hemlock bark from the Catskills was used for tanning leather. This leather was then sent to companies in New York City, Gloversville, and Johnstown. There it was made into shoes, gloves, saddles, and other products.

Because New York was changing so quickly into an industrial center, some felt its society needed to change, too. One issue concerned voting rights. Until 1821, the only people allowed to vote in national elections were men who owned property. In that year, voting rights were granted to all white men (free black men still had to own property to vote).

Many poor people still felt that they were treated unfairly. In New York, many working farmers rented their land from rich landowners who owned much of the farmland across the state. In 1839, some of them refused to pay their rent. Known as anti-renters, these farmers attacked landlords throughout the Mohawk

Inventor Elias Howe shows the speed of his sewing machine by racing five women who are sewing by hand (right). Howe's invention helped New York state become the nation's main clothing producer.

Both as a seaport and as a center of trading, New York City has been one of the nation's most important business centers. This illustration (below) shows what the city looked like at the start of the 19th century.

and Hudson valleys. Finally, during the 1840s, many landlords began breaking up their estates into small, independent farms.

By the middle of the 19th century, more and more women began speaking out for equal rights with men. At this time, women were not allowed to vote in elections. They were forbidden to own property. They also had no rights to keep their own children if their husbands left them.

Among those who spoke out was Elizabeth Cady Stanton. Her father was a judge, and Stanton had seen women come to him many times, asking for help after being abandoned by their husbands and left without money or their children. But because the laws did not protect women, there was nothing the judge could do.

In 1840, Stanton met Lucretia Mott, a well-known leader in the anti-slavery movement, and organized a meeting at her home in Seneca Falls, a small town in western New York, to discuss women's rights. These included the right to own property, to share the custody of children, to gain an education, and to have a career. Stanton realized that women could never achieve any of these rights without the right to vote. Over three hundred local residents attended this meeting, which came to be known as the Seneca Falls Convention. Of all the women there, only one, Charlotte Woodward, would live long enough to vote legally for the first time in 1920. But a movement began that would change the lives of their daughters and granddaughters.

New York honored those active in the fight to end slavery, both before and after the Civil War. In this drawing (right), the guns in the fort on Governor's Island in New York Harbor fire a salute as Frederick Douglass, a former slave and abolitionist, prepares to leave for Haiti.

In 1848, Elizabeth Stanton planned the first women's rights meeting ever held in the United States from this house (below, opposite page) in Seneca Falls, New York. Although Stanton argued then that women should be allowed to vote, women could not vote until 1920.

New York and the Civil War

Slavery was legal in New York up until 1827, although by that time few New Yorkers had slaves. In fact, some people in the North wanted to see slavery ended across the country.

Leading New York supporters of the antislavery movement were Henry Ward Beecher, Gerrit Smith, and Arthur and Lewis Tappen. They were called abolitionists. They joined antislavery societies, and some helped slaves escape from the South to Canada. Runaways would be hidden in an abolitionist's home until it was safe to guide him or her to freedom. These homes were called "stations," and those who helped were called "conductors" in an escape route known as the Underground Railroad.

One of the most important stopovers was Pultneyville, New York. Here, blacks were hidden until boats were ready to take them secretly across Lake Ontario into Canada. Many abolitionists risked their lives and broke the law to help slaves.

Two of the most important abolitionists were themselves freed slaves. Harriet Tubman had escaped from slavery, but instead of going to Canada, she decided to help other runaways. She personally led over 300 people through New York to Canada. Sojourner Truth was another former slave who became a hero in the fight to end slavery. After she had a religious vision in 1843, she changed her name from "Isabella Baumfree" to Sojourner Truth and toured the country, going to abolitionist rallies and preaching to her followers.

Another important New Yorker who spoke against slavery was Horace Greeley, who started the New York *Tribune*. Greeley's column was a popular section. In it, Greeley argued strongly for the end of slavery.

In the end, only the Civil War would stop slavery for good. After it broke out in 1861, New York sent more soldiers to the Union Army than any other state. Nearly 450,000 New Yorkers fought in the war and about 50,000 were killed. The first Northern officer to be killed, in fact, was Colonel Elmer Ellsworth of Mechanicville, New York. He was shot while pulling down a Confederate flag in a hotel in Alexandria, Virginia.

New York also gave weapons and supplies to the Union effort. Light and heavy cannons, rifles, and ammunition were made at Cold Spring, Ilion, and Watervliet. Schenectady made locomotives and other railroad equipment. Troy's iron works made horseshoes for the cavalry. Boots were made in Rochester. Mills all over the state ran day and night to make uniforms. And New York's rails and canals carried more freight than ever. Many New York industries grew very quickly during the war. Many business owners also grew rich.

For workers, prices went up but paychecks stayed the same. Rich people could avoid serving in the Union Army by paying $300, or paying someone else to take their place. But others who could not pay had to serve. Many working people grew angry about the war.

This anger exploded in July 1863. Thousands of poor workers rioted in the streets of New York City. They could not afford to buy their way out of the army. Also, they saw no reason to fight for the freedom of blacks in the South. They resented the city's blacks for getting work on the docks and in construction gangs—jobs that they needed.

The draft riots lasted three days, and over 50,000 people took part. Between 400 and 2,000 people were killed when rioters wrecked the city's draft headquarters, looted stores, and attacked abolitionists and blacks.

None of the Civil War's battles were fought in New York State. But the war changed everything. Many of the businessmen and bankers who had helped pay for the Union war effort were now more powerful than ever.

Many wealthy men paid others to serve for them. This practice angered many New Yorkers and led to the draft riots of 1863. This engraving (opposite, top) shows men lining up for a drawing to find out if they have to serve or not.

This photograph (right) shows several men who served as doctors in the Union Army's 164th New York Infantry group.

Rich and Poor

The years between the Civil War and the 20th century are known as the Gilded Age because so many owners of large companies became millionaires. After the Civil War, more and more goods were being made in factories. Hundreds of factories sprang up throughout the reunited nation. These factories needed money to get started. A lot of this money came from bankers and businessmen from New York City. These men became even richer as the factories began making more money. Among these men were millionaires John D. Rockefeller, Cornelius Vanderbilt, and Edward H. Harriman.

At the same time, new kinds of industries were replacing old ones. Some products, like brick, lumber, and salt, were being made more cheaply in other parts of the country. New York factories in these trades gradually closed down. Meanwhile, other new trades, like the clothing industry, grew very fast. In fact, the clothing trade soon became New York's biggest industry.

Other industries that grew quickly after the Civil War were printing and publishing. A New Yorker, Richard Hoe, had invented a new type of printing press in 1846. This machine made it possible to print more material than ever before.

The camera industry was born in New York State in the 1880s. That

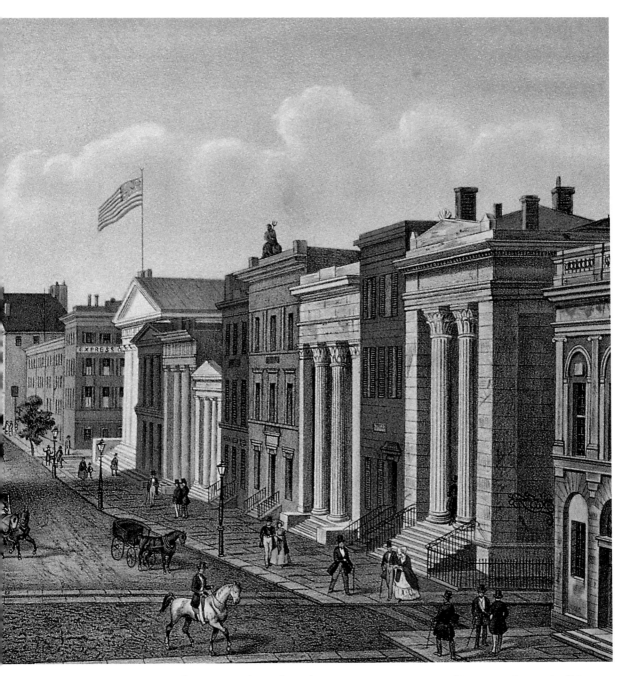

The New York Stock Exchange was organized in 1792 by twenty-four New Yorkers who met under a tree on downtown Manhattan's Wall Street. This scene shows Wall Street in about 1830. By 1900 Wall Street bankers such as J. P. Morgan had become as powerful as presidents.

was when George Eastman of Rochester began making roll film out of paper. (Before then, photo negatives were made of large glass plates.) Eastman began making and selling cameras to the public in 1888. He made photography into a popular hobby. Besides the camera, New York State was also a major supplier of such inventions as typewriters, sewing machines, and electrical equipment.

As all of these businesses grew, they needed more and more workers. New York's population likewise grew. Many people came to the state, arriving first in New York City. Many stayed in New York City, while others moved upstate to cities such as Rochester and Buffalo. By 1860, half of New York City's residents had been born in Europe—most of them Jews from Germany and Catholics from Ireland. Many Germans found work in the clothing industry. Eventually these German Jews came to run most of the clothing shops.

Because of their religion, the Irish Catholics found many jobs closed to them. They took what jobs they could find, often in construction and in shipyards.

After the Civil War, more of these newcomers, or immigrants, arrived. Starting in 1892, almost all passed through the immigration center at Ellis Island. Most of these immigrants now were either Italians or Eastern European Jews from nations such as Poland and Russia. Many Italians

found work on large construction projects such as the Brooklyn Bridge and the Statue of Liberty. Many Eastern Europeans also went to work in the clothing industry.

Meanwhile, companies were getting bigger. They grew into giant corporations when their owners bought up more and more factories and smaller businesses. Soon there was a huge gap between the very wealthy man who owned the company and the many poor workers who made the company's products. Usually the owner cared more about the money he was making than about the rights of his workers.

Two of the largest and most powerful companies during this time were the Standard Oil Company, owned by John D. Rockefeller, and United States Steel, owned by J. P. Morgan. These millionaires, and others, spent

This early advertisement (opposite, top) is for the Eastman-Kodak Company's popular Brownie camera. The company helped turn Rochester into a center of high technology. It is still one of the world's leaders in photography.

Between 1840 and 1910, many people from Europe arrived in the United States seeking a better life. Many families, like the one in this picture (right), settled in New York City. There they often found their new lives just as difficult as the ones they had left behind.

some of their money on art collections and luxuries. Morgan put together a great library of rare books and a painting collection containing several masterpieces. These can be seen in New York today in the Morgan Library. Perhaps his greatest treasures were his three yachts—*Corsair I*, *II*, and *III*. The last of these, at 302 feet, was longer than a football field. Someone once asked Morgan about the cost of this yacht. He answered, "Anybody that even has to think about the cost had better not get one." When Morgan died in 1913, he was worth about $68 million—a sum that did not even include the value of his art collection!

Politics

Ever since colonial times, New York has been an important center for government. In the 19th century, many national political leaders came from Albany and New York. Martin Van Buren, for example, served as a senator and then governor for New York State. Later he became Andrew Jackson's vice president, and then president himself.

At the center of New York City politics was a group known as Tammany Hall, which was started just two weeks after the signing of the U.S. Constitution. It was named after a legendary Delaware Indian chief who was thought to have wisdom and a great love for liberty. In the begin-

ning, Tammany's members even called their leaders sachems, just as the Iroquois had done years earlier.

At first, Tammany was a voice for the poorer classes in the city. The group fought to change the election rules, so that people who didn't own property could still vote. They did not succeed, but they joined together to buy enough property to vote in the elections of 1800 and 1801.

The group was against many of Governor De Witt Clinton's plans, including the Erie Canal. They continued to support the working class. Then, in 1821, when election rules were changed so that the working class could vote, Tammany Hall

became a powerful force in politics. In fact, for the rest of the 19th century, any candidate Tammany supported was guaranteed to win.

As time went on, the members of Tammany Hall began using their power for their own profit. They found ways to steal money from the city government. Even if they got into trouble, they could avoid going to jail because of their links to Tammany.

Within Tammany Hall there were often struggles for power. In 1829, for example, a number of Tammany supporters split off to form the Working Men's Party. They were known as Workies. They spoke out for better conditions for the working class.

Tammany Hall's power reached its peak in the period after the Civil War. By 1868, Tammany controlled the

For over 100 years, New York City politics were controlled by a group known as Tammany Hall. Although Tammany politicians worked to help the city's poorer citizens, they often used their power dishonestly. In 1868, the Democratic Party met at Tammany Hall's headquarters (above) to pick its candidate for president.

The Workies supported better wages and conditions for New York's poorer classes. They printed this cartoon (opposite page) in the 1830s to show their distrust for Tammany Hall—which is being promoted by the devil, while Liberty favors the workers.

entire state government. It supported Horatio Seymour running for president, and the Democratic Convention of 1868 was held at Tammany Hall headquarters.

From 1865 to 1872, Tammany Hall was run by William Marcy Tweed, who was supported by both the city's rich and its immigrant voters. Tweed controlled both the city and state governments. During his years in power, Tweed and his men stole almost $200 million. They set up a system ("Tweed's Ring") within the city government by bribing many New York politicians. Any company that sold services or supplies to the city had to charge twice as much. Half of the money would then go to Tweed and his partners. Under this system, the city paid almost $2 million to have a single building plastered, and almost $200,000 for forty chairs and tables.

Finally, Tweed and his men got into trouble for their actions. In 1871, they were tried and convicted, thanks to the efforts of Samuel Tilden, who later became governor. Tilden, a member of Tammany himself, was perhaps the most important Democrat to call for the reform of Tammany Hall and the Democratic Party. Later he ran for president. But it was also the cartoons of Thomas Nast that helped bring Tweed down. Nast's regular cartoons ran in *Harper's Weekly* magazine. They often pointed out Tweed's corrupt ways. Tweed

tried to pay Nast so he would stop the cartoons, but Nast would not be bought. His cartoons made the crimes of Tweed's Ring public, and helped to bring about its end. Before long, Tweed and Tammany Hall were a national disgrace.

Tammany Hall was exposed, but it did not change overnight. Over the next several decades, a new group of criminals took over the group. Even as reformers watched Tammany Hall's every move, the party regained power under John Kelly, who went by the nickname Honest John. Kelly was just as dishonest as Tweed had been, but he was more careful in concealing his crimes.

Although Tammany Hall continued to control New York City, it had lost its power in state politics. In 1883, a Democrat was elected governor, but he was not connected to Tammany Hall at all. He was Grover Cleveland. As governor, Cleveland refused to allow Tammany Hall to interfere in state business. Later he became president, serving for two terms.

It took a long time and much effort to put Tammany Hall down for good. The state government had three separate investigations. The Tammany crimes continued into the next century. Important New York leaders, including future U.S. president Theodore Roosevelt, fought against Tammany's influence. But it wasn't until the 1930s that Tammany finally lost all of its power.

Perhaps the most dishonest head of Tammany Hall was William Marcy "Boss" Tweed. The cartoons of Thomas Nast, like this one (right), helped put Tweed and his partners in jail.

Theodore Roosevelt, who later became president of the United States, served as president of New York City's police board beginning in 1895. Roosevelt was determined to end corruption (as shown in this cartoon, below), even though Tammany Hall tried to stop him.

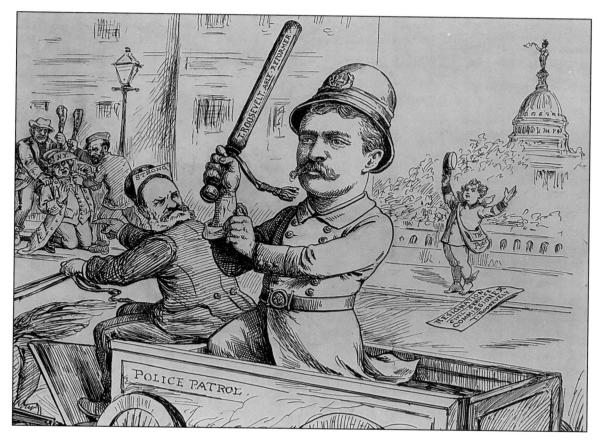

Into a New Century

The 20th century brought many changes to New York. The state grew even more important as a transportation center. The most famous airplane voyage in New York history took place in 1927. Charles A. Lindbergh flew from Roosevelt Field (in Long Island) to Paris and started the age of air travel.

New York was a leader in putting new inventions and systems to use. In the early 1920s, the first radio station was started. New York was the first state to build broadcasting stations. Soon it became the center for most radio networks, which broadcast programs throughout the nation.

Radio broadcasting could not exist without the work of Thomas Alva Edison. Edison invented the electric light bulb, and set up the first electrical generating station, on Manhattan's Pearl Street. Electricity could now be used for many purposes. Elevators could be built. And with elevators, buildings could be built higher and higher. Many of New York City's most famous buildings, like the Empire State Building and the Chrysler Building, would never have been built without elevators to carry people to the top floors.

Electricity also brought in faster street cars. These replaced the steam-powered trains that rode on elevated tracks above the city streets. Electric

By the start of the 20th century, many people had made their fortunes on Wall Street. This photo (left) shows the inside of the New York Stock Exchange as it appeared in 1908.

Leading supporters of the women's right to vote marched down New York City's Fifth Avenue in 1917 (right). Women won the right to vote in New York that year, three years before it became the law across the country.

power also led to the first subway trains in 1904.

Up until the turn of the century, Brooklyn, Queens, Staten Island, and the Bronx were separate cities. People began to talk about combining them all with New York City. Andrew Haswell Green promoted this idea, and, in 1898, his idea won. New York City went from being just Manhattan, with its 2 million residents, to a city made up of five "boroughs" (as the separate towns were now called) and 3.5 million people.

These events were a great concern for most New Yorkers. But suddenly all eyes were turned to a crisis in Europe. In 1917, America entered World War I, which was being fought in France and Germany. Once again,

New York played an important part in the country's war effort. Most of the 2 million soldiers left for Europe from New York Harbor. New York also supplied more war materials than any other state. Its citizens bought one fourth of all war bonds that the government sold, and gave more money to the Red Cross and other relief groups. The state sent more soldiers, marines, and sailors to the armed forces than any other state. Over 500,000 men were drafted and about 14,000 were killed.

During the 1920s, the spirit of reform was stronger than ever in New York. Workers' lives improved because of the efforts of Governor Alfred E. Smith. During four terms as governor, Smith fought for laws to shorten

working hours and give more money to workers who had been injured on the job. He also improved schools, and built new hospitals, roads, bridges, and parks.

New York in the 1920s continued to grow and prosper. Following the World War, the state's bankers began to lend money not just to American businesses, but to businesses around the world. The two major stock exchanges on Wall Street, the New York Stock Exchange and the Curb (later renamed the American Stock Exchange) became the most powerful trading places in the world.

New York City became the nation's center of arts and culture. During the 1920s, sixty theaters were active in the city, showing plays, musical comedies, and famous revues like the Zeigfeld Follies. Never before had New York been so alive with artists and writers.

Many of these artists and writers were African Americans. During the 1920s many blacks moved from the Southern states to settle in big Northern cities like Chicago, Philadelphia, and especially New York—in Harlem, at the northern end of Manhattan. Before long, Harlem was not only the most heavily populated black neighborhood in New York City, but the center of African-American culture for the whole nation.

Jazz musicians such as Cab Calloway, singers such as Josephine Baker and Billie Holliday, and writers such as Langston Hughes all became

During the 1920s, jazz was America's favorite music. Jazz was especially popular in Harlem, where many nightclubs attracted people from all over New York City. Opposite is King Oliver's band, featuring a young trumpet player named Louis Armstrong.

Fiorella La Guardia (left) was New York City's mayor from 1934 to 1945. While in office, he built better parks and new houses, and ended the dishonest rule of Tammany Hall politicians.

famous in the 1920s. Harlem was known as a wild, free-spirited place. Many whites went to Harlem's clubs for dancing and music. Langston Hughes wrote that the 1920s was a time "when the Negro was in vogue."

All New Yorkers suffered when the Great Depression struck America and other industrial nations. This worldwide economic collapse was caused by many factors. One was the failure of the stock market on Wall Street in 1929. Millionaires lost fortunes when their holdings suddenly became worthless. Many companies closed, and thousands of workers throughout the country lost their jobs.

Luckily for New Yorkers, the new governor cared about helping all of the state's citizens. His name was Franklin Delano Roosevelt. Soon after taking office, Governor Roosevelt set up jobs for the unemployed and passed laws to help the poor and to improve work conditions.

In 1933, Franklin Roosevelt became president of the nation and helped lead America out of the Depression. Back in New York, other leaders stepped in. Fiorello LaGuardia was New York's mayor from 1934 to 1945. La Guardia was famous for roaming New York City streets in search of ways to make things better. He hounded gangsters and fought against Tammany Hall. LaGuardia made many improvements in the lives of New York City's people. He built better parks and new housing, and cleared away slums.

New York in a Changing World

When Japanese planes bombed Pearl Harbor in 1941, America entered World War II. New York sent over 1 million of its citizens to fight. More than 38,000 were killed.

Factories across the state turned out electrical machines, airplanes, and ships. Buffalo became famous for making fighter planes and military transport planes. Syracuse manufactured guns, shells, and iron products. Cameras, periscopes, and scientific instruments came from Rochester.

With industry producing so much for the war effort, the Depression ended. This prosperity continued for ten years in New York after the war ended in 1945. New York grew more quickly than ever before. During the 1950s, Governor Thomas Dewey built the New York State Thruway and created the state's public university system. In 1961, the state built a hydroelectric plant at Niagara Falls, which brought cheaper power rates and helped local industries.

Another major event of the postwar era was the opening of the St. Lawrence Seaway in 1959. The Seaway allows oceangoing ships to travel directly from the Great Lakes to the Atlantic Ocean. But because ships can now bypass Buffalo and Rochester, these cities have lost much of their importance as transportation centers.

New York's governor in the 1960s was Nelson Rockefeller. He added many new schools to the state university system and put more money into state health care. At this time, many newcomers moved to New York City. More blacks came up from the South. A large number of immigrants arrived from Puerto Rico. Many of these people had trouble finding work, and the number of New Yorkers without jobs grew. The poor areas of the city soon became overcrowded. Tensions between groups living in these neighborhoods sometimes turned violent as many people competed for the same jobs. Today, mistrust and anger between different races and religions continue to be problems in the cities in New York State.

At the same time, New York City has also made a major contribution to world peace. In 1946, the United Nations was started with the help of John D. Rockefeller, Jr., who gave

Many tourists visit Adirondack State Park year-round to enjoy beautiful views of its mountains, lakes, and forests (opposite, top).

During the past twenty years, many Indian rights groups, such as the Indian Defense League (right), have been formed to improve the lives of these original New Yorkers.

$8.5 million to the new organization. Diplomats and ambassadors from around the world meet at U.N. headquarters in New York City to find solutions to worldwide problems.

Since 1945, the world has changed at a much faster pace than ever before. New York State has suffered as more and more industries have moved south and west, where land is cheaper and more plentiful. Buffalo in particular has faced painful changes. But some factors are now working in its favor: It is still the world's leading flour-milling city. It has also recently benefited from a free trade pact with Canada, which has brought Buffalo business and renewed prosperity .

New York City also has a growing list of troubles. By the 1970s, the city began having serious trouble paying for roads, bridges, and public housing. As the population became poorer, the city raised less and less money from taxes. Although New York City often turns to Albany for extra money, the state government is not always willing or able to pay. In fact, ever since the days of Tammany Hall, many of New York's upstate residents have felt that New York City has not been careful in spending its money. In 1975, the United States government had to step in to help.

One growing industry in the state is tourism. New York has many natural attractions, which draw visitors from other areas. Places such as Niagara Falls and the Finger Lakes help bring many visitors into the state, which in turn provides more jobs for the local residents.

One of New York's greatest parks is the Adirondack State Park. It is the largest state park in America, totaling more than 2 million acres.

Some people want to build more houses and resorts on Adirondack land, arguing that the region needs the money these projects would bring in. Others want the wilderness to be left alone. They point out that the Adirondacks are already threatened by pollution.

Of all the different groups of people who have lived in New York, the Indians have seen the greatest changes. In just three centuries, New York has changed from a land of forests and wilderness into a bustling state with large cities and farms. Today, some New York Indians live on reservations, large areas of land set aside by the U.S. government. Clashes have occured between the government and the Indians over this land. Like the state parks, reservations are in danger from pollution.

New York has faced many challenges in its history as a state. But it has always been able to respond well to difficult times. Over the centuries, it has welcomed many different kinds of people. The leaders of New York State have struggled to find ways to bring all these different people together, and to solve ongoing problems. As the world changes faster and faster, all New Yorkers are challenged to keep searching for new solutions.

New York City's World Trade Center (above), which was begun in 1966 and finished in 1980, is 110 stories high, making it the world's second tallest building. Only the Sears Tower, in Chicago, is taller.

In 1989, David Dinkins (opposite page) was elected mayor of New York City. As New York's first African-American mayor, he has fought hard to bring New Yorkers of different backgrounds together.

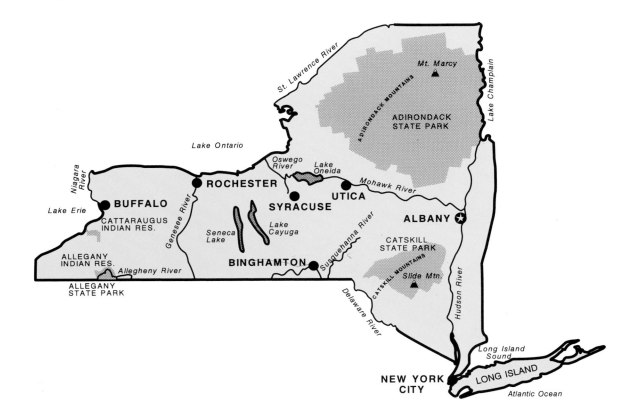

Land area:

49,108 square miles, of which 1,884 are inland water. Thirtieth largest state.

Major rivers:

The Susquehanna; the Delaware; the Hudson; the Mohawk; the Genesee; the Oswego; the Seneca; the Niagara; the St. Lawrence; the Allegheny.

Highest point: Mt. Marcy, 5,344 ft.

Major bodies of water:

Lake Erie; Lake Ontario; Lake George; Lake Champlain; Lake Cayuga; Lake Seneca; Lake Oneida; Chautauqua Lake; Long Island Sound.

Climate:

Average January temperature: 21°F
Average July temperature: 69°F

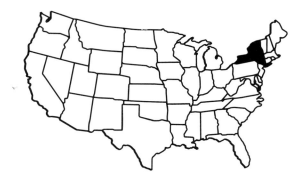

Population: 17,990,455 (1990)
Rank: 2nd
    1900: 7,268,894
    1790: 340,120

Population of major cities (1990):

New York City	7,322,564
Buffalo	328,123
Rochester	231,636
Yonkers	188,082
Syracuse	163,860
Albany	101,082

Ethnic breakdown by percentage (1990):

White	74.4%
[includes Hispanic	1.2%]
African American	15.9%
Asian	3.9%
American Indian	0.3%
Other	5.5%

Economy:
Banking and finance, printing and publishing, public relations, communications, agriculture, manufacturing (clothing; scientific instruments, electrical equipment, and machinery), mining, and tourism.

State Government:
Legislature: Made up of the 61-member Senate and the 150-member Assembly. Both senators and assembly members serve 2-year terms.
Governor: The governor, who is elected for a 4-year term, heads the executive branch.
Courts: New York consists of 12 judicial districts. The court of appeals is the highest court in the state, hearing cases only from the appellate division of the supreme court.

State Flag

Two figures, Justice and Liberty, stand on each side of the state's coat of arms. At the top, an American eagle takes flight from an image of the globe. In the middle is a landscape, showing the rising sun and two sailboats. New York adoped this design for the flag in 1909.

State Seal

The seal for New York closely follows the design for the flag. As in the flag, two sailboats are coming together on a river, as the sun rises over the mountain behind them. The word "Excelsior," New York's motto, appears in a scroll at the bottom.

State Motto

Since 1778, New York's motto has been "Excelsior." This word means "higher," and is an expression for progress.

State Nickname

The "Empire State"; sometimes also called the "Knickerbocker State."

Places

Adirondack State Park, Newcomb

Albany Institute of History and Art, Albany

American Museum of Natural History, New York City

Asia Society Gallery, New York City

Bill of Rights Museum, Mt. Vernon

Brooklyn Children's Museum, Brooklyn

Catskill Mountain Railroad, Mt. Pleasant

Center for African Art, New York City

Chinatown History Museum, New York City

Fillmore Glen State Park, Moravia

Fort Delaware Museum of Colonial History, Narrowsburg

Fort William Henry, Lake George

FDR National Historic Site, Hyde Park

Genesee Country Museum, Rochester

George Eastman House, Rochester

Gilbert Lake State Park, Oneonta

Glimmerglass State Park, Cooperstown

Grafton Lakes State Park, Grafton

Harriet Tubman Home, Auburn

Ice Caves Mountain and Sam's Point, Ellenville

Intrepid Museum, New York City

Iroquois Indian Museum, Schoharie

The Jewish Museum, New York City

to See

Jones Beach State Park, Wantagh

The Metropolitan Museum of Art, New York City

Museo del Barrio, New York City

Museum of Cartoon Art, Rye Brook

Museum of the Hudson Highlands, Cornwall-on-Hudson

The Museum of Modern Art, New York City

National Baseball Hall of Fame, Cooperstown

National Museum of Dance, Saratoga

National Museum of Racing, Saratoga

National Soccer Hall of Fame, Oneonta

The National Women's Hall of Fame, Seneca Falls

New York Botanical Garden, Bronx

New York State Museum, Albany

Niagara Falls Convention and Visitors Bureau, Niagara Falls

Queens County Farm Museum, Queens

Richmondtown Restoration, Staten Island

Sapsucker Woods, Ithaca

Saratoga National Historical Park, Stillwater

Statue of Liberty, New York City

Stony Point Battlefield, Stony Point

Sonnenberg Estate, Canandaigua

Susan B. Anthony Home, Rochester

State Flower

New York's legislature adopted the rose as the state flower in 1955. This popular and fragrant flower appears in several different colors, including red, white, pink, yellow, and violet. Roses of all colors are honored in New York.

State Bird

The bluebird was named New York's official bird in 1970. Found throughout the Eastern and Southern parts of America, these tiny, brightly colored birds were nicknamed blue robins by early settlers.

State Tree

In 1956, the sugar maple was made New York's state tree. The tree's sap is gathered in the early spring and made into maple sugar products such as candy and syrup.

New York History

1524 Giovanni da Verrazano explores New York Harbor

1570 Iroquois League of Five Nations forms

1609 Henry Hudson explores the Hudson River

1625 New Amsterdam founded by the Dutch

1654 The first Jews arrive in New Amsterdam

1664 England gains control of New Amsterdam, renaming it New York

1689 Jacob Leisler's Rebellion

1735 John Peter Zenger trial

1754 Meeting of the Albany Congress

1776 The Battle of Long Island: British occupy New York City

1777 The Battle of Saratoga
• New York adopts its first constitution

1784 New York City named U.S. capital

1788 New York becomes 11th state

1789 The Society of Tammany is created

1792 The Stock Exchange is started in New York City

1797 Albany is named state capital

1807 Robert Fulton invents first steamboat, the *Clermont*

1811 Founding of Rochester

1813 The Battle of Lake Erie

1814 The Battle of Lake Champlain

American

1492 Christopher Columbus reaches America

1607 Jamestown (Virginia) founded by English colonists

1620 *Mayflower* arrives at Plymouth (Massachusetts)

1754–63 French and Indian War

1765 Parliament passes Stamp Act

1775–83 Revolutionary War

1776 Signing of the Declaration of Independence

1788–90 First congressional elections

1791 Bill of Rights added to U.S. Constitution

1803 Louisiana Purchase

1812–14 War of 1812

1820 Missouri Compromise

1836 Battle of the Alamo, Texas

1846–48 Mexican-American War

1849 California Gold Rush

1860 South Carolina secedes from Union

1861–65 Civil War

1862 Lincoln signs Homestead Act

1863 Emancipation Proclamation

1865 President Lincoln assassinated (April 14)

1865–77 Reconstruction in the South

1866 Civil Rights bill passed

1881 President James Garfield shot (July 2)

History

1896 First Ford automobile is made

1898–99 Spanish-American War

1901 President William McKinley is shot in Buffalo (Sept. 6)

1917 U.S. enters World War I

1922 Nineteenth Amendment passed, giving women the vote

1929 U.S. stock market crash; Great Depression begins

1933 Franklin D. Roosevelt becomes president; begins New Deal recovery programs

1941 Japanese attack Pearl Harbor (Dec. 7); U.S. enters World War II

1945 U.S. drops atomic bomb on Hiroshima and Nagasaki; Japan surrenders, ending World War II

1963 President John Kennedy assassinated (Nov. 22)

1964 Civil Rights Act passed

1965–73 Vietnam War

1968 Martin Luther King, Jr., shot in Memphis (April 4)

1974 President Richard Nixon resigns because of Watergate break-in scandal

1979–81 Hostage crisis in Iran: 52 Americans held captive for 444 days

1989 End of U.S.-Soviet cold war

1991 Gulf War

1992 U.S. sends marines to Somalia

New York History

1817–25 Building of the Erie Canal

1827 Slavery is abolished in the state

1830 Beginning of the Mormon church in Palmyra

1845 Farmers' "anti-rent" strike

1848 Seneca Falls Convention

1851 The *New York Times* is founded

1863 New York City antidraft riots

1883 Opening of the Brooklyn Bridge

1888 George Eastman invents the Kodak camera

1909 Founding of the National Association for the Advancement of Colored People (N.A.A.C.P.) in New York City

1911 Triangle Shirtwaist Company fire in New York City: 146 workers are killed

1952 United Nations headquarters finished in New York City

1954–59 St. Lawrence Seaway constructed

1960 New York State Thruway completed

1974 Opening of the World Trade Center

1975–76 New York City faces grave financial crisis

1989 David Dinkins becomes New York City's first black mayor

1992 Democratic Convention in New York City nominates Bill Clinton for president

Hiawatha (c. 1525–c. 1575) This Indian leader helped start the Iroquois Confederacy.

Henry Hudson (?–1611) This English captain explored New York Bay and the Hudson River in 1609 and claimed the land there for the Dutch.

Peter Stuyvesant (1592–1672) This Dutch governor ruled the New Netherland colony from 1647 to 1664.

Captain William Kidd (c. 1645–1701) This wealthy sea captain turned to piracy off the coast of Africa in 1696.

Joseph Brant (1742–1807) A Mohawk leader, Brant (Thayendanegea) was an important British ally. After the Revolution, the British gave Brant and his followers land along the Grand River in Ontario, Canada.

Joseph Brant

Margaret Cochran Corbin (1751–c. 1800) Corbin was the first woman to fight in the Revolutionary War. When her husband was killed at his cannon post, "Captain Molly" took over and kept firing until she was wounded by a shot in the arm.

Alexander Hamilton (c. 1757–1804) This speaker, writer, and lawyer helped shape the foundation of the United States by helping write the Constitution.

Martin Van Buren (1782–1862) The 8th president of the U.S. was born in the town of Kinderhook. He ran again in 1848 for the Free Soil Party, but was defeated.

Washington Irving (1783–1859) The first American-born writer to earn a successful living from his writing, Irving (born in New York City) is best known for his stories "Rip Van Winkle" and "The Legend of Sleepy Hollow."

Sojourner Truth (1797–1883) This powerful speaker and social reformer was born a slave in Ulster County. She took to the road to speak out against slavery.

Elizabeth Cady Stanton (1815–1902) One of the founders of the American women's rights movement, Stanton organized the Seneca Falls Convention in 1848.

Walt Whitman (1819–92) Born in West Hills, Whitman is best known for his book of poetry, *Leaves of Grass.* He was also a reporter and editor, and a hospital volunteer during the Civil War.

Jay Gould

Jay Gould (1836–92) This banker triggered the "Black Friday" financial panic in 1869 when he tried to seize total control of the New York City gold market.

William James (1842–1910)
Born in New York City, William James taught philosophy and psychology at Harvard University. He is known as one of the nation's greatest thinkers.

Henry James (1843–1916)
William's younger brother Henry was one of the country's leading novelists.

Elihu Root (1845–1937)
Born in Clinton, Root became famous when he prosecuted "Boss" Tweed. In 1912, Root won the Nobel Peace Prize.

Theodore Roosevelt (1858–1919) Roosevelt was elected New York's governor in 1898. He was vice president in 1900 and became the 26th president in 1901, after McKinley's assassination in Buffalo.

Grandma Moses (1860–1961) Born Anna Mary Robertson, Grandma Moses began painting rural New York scenes at the age of 76. Her work has been shown at the Museum of Modern Art.

Edith Wharton (1862–1937)
Born and raised in New York City, Wharton wrote many novels about the upper classes.

Charles Evans Hughes (1862–1948) Born in Glens Falls, Hughes served as governor of New York, and in 1930 became Chief Justice of the U.S. Supreme Court.

Franklin Delano Roosevelt (1882–1945) Born in Hyde Park, Roosevelt was a lawyer and a New York State senator. In 1929 he became governor of New York, and in 1932 he was elected 32nd president, the first to serve four terms.

Eugene O'Neill (1888–1953) O'Neill was born in New York City. He overcame a difficult childhood to become one of the greatest American playwrights. His plays include "A Moon for the Misbegotten," "Anna Christie," and "Long Day's Journey into Night."

Lou Gehrig (1903–41) Lou Gehrig was signed in 1925 by the New York Yankees. He hit .340, with 493 home runs. He was forced to retire by a rare muscle illness that is known today as Lou Gehrig's Disease.

Jonas Salk (b. 1914) This New York City doctor developed the first effective vaccine against polio in 1953. He later tried to find a cure for cancer.

Shirley Chisholm

Shirley Chisholm (b. 1924)
Shirley Chisholm was born in Brooklyn. In 1968, she became the first black woman elected to the House of Representatives. In 1972, she was also the first black woman to run for president, winning 10% of the Democratic Convention votes.

Malcolm X (1925–65)
Malcolm X became famous as the minister of the Black Muslim's Harlem mosque. In 1963, he left the Nation of Islam to found a rival group. He was assassinated in Harlem two years later.

General Colin Powell (b. 1936) Army general Colin Powell, born in New York City, became the first African American to serve as chairman of the joint chiefs of staff.

Pictures in this volume:

Buffalo/Erie County Historical Society: 51 (bottom)

Culver Pictures: 11 (top)

Eastman Kodak Company: 41 (top)

Library of Congress: 7, 9 (both), 11 (bottom), 13, 14, 15, 17, 18, 19 (both), 21, 22, 23 (both), 25, 26, 27, 29, 30, 31, 33 (top), 35, 37 (both), 39, 41 (bottom), 42, 43, 45 (both), 46, 47, 49

National Archives: 24, 48

National Women's Rights Historic Park: 34

New York Historical Society: 28, 33 (bottom)

New York State Dept. of Economic Development: 2, 51 (top)

Office of the Mayor, City of New York: 52

World Trade Center: 53

About the authors:

Monique Avakian is a Boston-based freelance writer and editor. She attended Beloit College in Wisconsin, where she won the Von Veschen-Steele award for excellence in education. She is the author of *The Meiji Restoration: the Rise of Modern Japan*, for Silver Burdett & Ginn.

Carter Smith III is an editor and writer living in the Boston area with his wife, Monique Avakian, and their daughter. He has written several other history books, including *One Giant Leap for Mankind* and *The Pyramid Builders*, both for Silver Burdett & Ginn. He grew up in New York City and is a graduate of Beloit College in Wisconsin.

Suggested reading:

Carpenter, Allan, *The Enchantment of America: New York*, Chicago: Childrens Press, 1978

Dudley, Bronson, *The Story of New York: Indian Territory to Empire State*, New York: Grosset & Dunlap, 1968

Fradin, Dennis B., *The New York Colony*, Chicago: Childrens Press, 1988

The Gateway States: Time-Life Library of America, New York: Time, Inc., 1968

Glassman, Bruce, *New York: The Great Cities Library*, New York: Blackbirch Press, in association with Rosen Publications, 1991

McCall, Barbara A., *Indian Tribes of America: The Iroquois*, Vero Beach, FL: Rourke Publications, 1989

Wolfson, Evelyn, *The Iroquois*, Brookfield, CT: The Millbrook Press, 1992

For more information contact:

New York State Historical Association
P.O. Box 800
Cooperstown, NY 13326
Tel. (607) 547-2533
Fax (607) 547-5384

New York State Department of Commerce
Division of Tourism
1 Commerce Plaza
Albany, NY 12245
Tel. (800) 225-5697

INDEX

Page numbers in *italics* indicate illustrations